W9-AHK-336

To:

....

From:

....

West Side Publishing is a division of Publications International, Ltd.

Copyright © 2009 Publications International, Ltd.
All rights reserved. This book may not be reproduced or quoted in whole or
in part by any means whatsoever without written permission from:

Louis Weber, CEO
Publications International, Ltd.
7373 North Cicero Avenue
Lincolnwood, Illinois 60712

Permission is never granted for commercial purposes.

ISBN-13: 978-1-4127-1584-3
ISBN-10: 1-4127-1584-9

Manufactured in China.

8 7 6 5 4 3 2 1

Kids Say the Cutest
Things About
Teachers

Illustrations by Amanda Haley

WEST
SIDE
PUBLISHING

A teacher's most important job is to put smartness in kids' heads.

Asher, age 7

I want to be a teacher
because you get to sit in
a comfortable chair.

Maisie, age 8

If there were no teachers,
school would be a zoo.

Clio, age 7

A person becomes
a teacher by asking
the principal.

Cameron, age 7

A teacher's main job is to
help you go potty when
you have to go.

Stella, age 3

The funny thing about teachers is they never have to go to the bathroom.

Natalie, age 8

Just when I learned to spell "January," my teacher changed the calendar to February.

Mary, age 7

If you want to be a
teacher, you have to love
talking and stickers.

Maya, age 6

I saw my teacher at the grocery store on a Saturday. It was weird, because I thought she lived at school and ate dinner in the cafeteria.

Matt, age 8

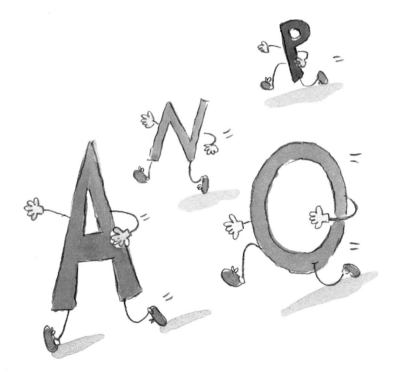

When my teacher erases
the board, where do the
words go?

James, age 5

If you want to become a
teacher, you have to take
an eight-hour quiz.

Olivia, age 7

One thing I've noticed
is that teachers love to
wear clothes that say
they're teachers.

Jennifer, age 8

My teacher told me to put on my thinking cap, but I never got one.

Devon, age 7

Grading is the hardest part of being a teacher, 'cause there aren't that many letters to choose from.

Grace, age 8

When we are reading together, my teacher tastes the pages before she turns them.

Teondra, age 6

Without teachers,
school would be called
"The Playpen."

Ethan, age 7

If you're a mom or dad
and want to know how
your kid is doing in
school, you go to a
parent-teacher concert.

Quinn, age 6

How do teachers come up
with the hard questions
on tests? I bet they use
the Internet.

Shane, age 8

My teacher told us how
the Pilgrims came to
America on a cauliflower.

David, age 5

Teachers do a lot of stuff
when they're not in school.
In summer, they barbecue.
In winter, they have
snowball fights.

Asher, age 7

If there were no teachers, we would be dumb and not know anything. People would ask, "What is your name?" and you might not know the answer.

McKayla, age 9

HELLO. My name is

?

My teacher told me my shoes were on the wrong feet. Whose feet did she think they were on?

Michael, age 7

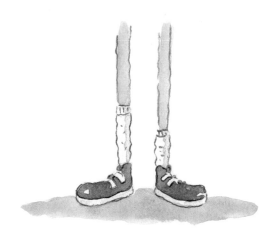

You can't learn everything from your teacher. You have to learn some things at recess—like how to play kickball, chase girls, and talk to the fifth graders.

Ben, age 8

CLASS RULES: Raise your hand. Sit in your

I wouldn't want to be a teacher, because I don't like to yell at kids.

Jaylen, age 7

inside voices, No pushing. No running in class.

Teaching is hard work. You have to make the kids have self-control.

Kayla, age 9

A teacher is a person who takes away your recess when you pass a note.

DaJeal, age 10

My teacher has the best cursive. She probably uses magic chalk.

Rodney, age 6

A teacher is a healthy,
well-grown person who
works really hard.

Marta, age 7

The hardest part of being a teacher is the teaching part.

Austin, age 8

DESERT

I hate practicing spelling. You miss one letter and the whole word's wrong.

Monique, age 6

My teacher said we should raise our hands if we have to go to the bathroom, but that doesn't help.

Derek, age 6

When they're not in school, teachers drive cool cars and eat egg salad.

Dominik, age 8

On my birthday, I wished there wouldn't be a test. I guess my teacher didn't get the message.

Sarah, age 9

My teacher says we're not allowed in the teachers' lounge. I bet they have a Ping-Pong table in there and free doughnuts.

Nathan, age 7

My teacher loves ABC order. We sit in ABC order. We line up in ABC order. I wonder if she calls her kids to dinner in ABC order.

Sloane, age 7

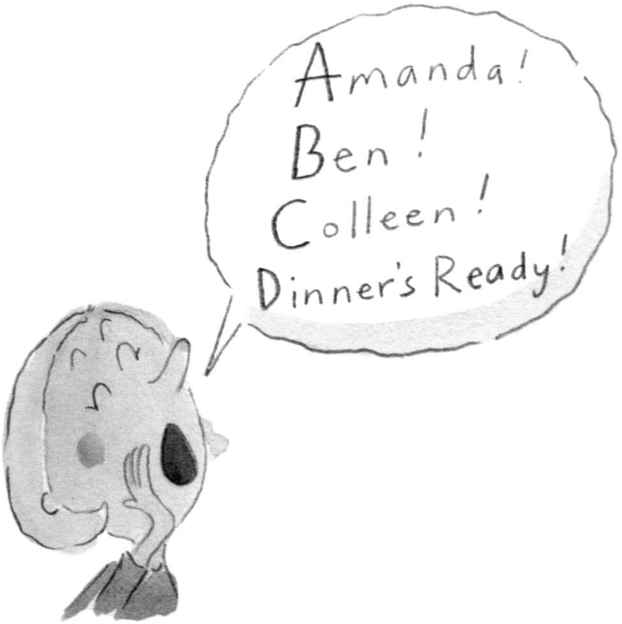
Amanda!
Ben!
Colleen!
Dinner's Ready!

If there were no teachers, there would be no homework. There would be recess all the time. There would be a party with a piñata. There would be dogs and cats.

Madeline, age 9

My teacher always says
to do your best, so I do
my best to stay out on the
playground all day!

Anthony, age 9

I want to be a teacher,
because it would be fun
to be nice to the kid you
were once.

Flora, age 7

Amanda Haley graduated from The School of the Art Institute of Chicago with a BFA in painting and drawing. She has illustrated more than 40 children's books, including both fictional and educational titles. Haley lives in Virginia with her husband, Brian, and dog, Mayzie.

Publications International, Ltd., wishes to thank the following schools for their submissions to *Kids Say the Cutest Things About Teachers*: Brennermann School (Chicago, IL), Bush Elementary School (Fulton, MO), Conn-West Elementary School (Grandview, MO), Gilkey Elementary School (Plainwell, MI), Holy Family School (Granite City, IL), Kennedy Middle School (Kankakee, IL), King Lab Magnet School (Evanston, IL), Plantation Park Elementary School (Plantation, FL), St. Agatha Catholic Academy (Chicago, IL), Starr Elementary School (Plainwell, MI)